Watchet
September 2006.

Legends & Folklore of Watchet

A miscellany of legends, quaint old customs, and anecdotes of a small harbour town.

Watchet has always been rich in character and characters, and some of the latter are featured on the following pages.

Having been passed down by word of mouth, one or two of the legends or tales may need to be taken with a pinch of salt. As to which is for the reader to decide—as a man once muttered sotto voce, "You pays yer money and you takes yer choice!"

Butcher Hooper's shop, Swain Street, in the 1880s.

Back cover: Watchet Town Crier Alec Danby.

Legends & Folklore of Watchet

W. H. (Ben) Norman

Published by W. H. (Ben) Norman ©
Lyn Cottage, Mill Lane, Watchet, Somerset, TA23 0AR.

By the same author: *Tales of Watchet Harbour*

First published 1992

© W. H. (BEN) NORMAN

ISBN 0 95 10842 1 6

3rd Reprint 2005

ACKNOWLEDGEMENTS

I am grateful to many friends who have helped in various ways with this book.

Special thanks to Derek Quint for his contribution of "The Ghosts of Watchet Town" (with haunting music) and his humorous drawings. Also to Dr. Glyn Court for permission to include "Lady Wyndham's Return," written in rhyme by his uncle, the late Rev. Lewis H. Court.

Printed by Colourtone Print & Graphics, Taunton, Somerset

CONTENTS

*The above anecdotes have appeared individually in local periodicals: *Exmoor Review* and *West Country Home and Leisure*.

DEDICATION

To my sister Edna Dixon.

PART 1 — LEGENDS

ST. DECUMAN AND HIS COW

Watchet's oldest legend goes way back to early in the fifth century and starts in Wales.

At that time a Celtic missionary, one St. Decuman, was made aware by travellers that the people of Watchet were heathen and in urgent need of spiritual guidance. St. Decuman was rather perturbed on hearing this and after giving the matter some thought, he decided to sail across the channel to Watchet to preach the gospel and thus to save the people from their wicked ways.

He bravely set out on a flimsy raft made of saplings and hides and, being very partial to a drink of milk, he took with him his own pet cow.

At Watchet he started building a church on a hill overlooking the town and then began to preach. He found the local people very unfriendly and unhelpful. For no known reason they took a dislike to him and one day 'one of them' chopped off his head with a hatchet.

Now, *according to the legend,* St. Decuman was quite unruffled when this happened. In a calm and saintly way he stooped and picked up his severed head. After washing off the blood in a nearby holy well, he popped it on again and, without any show of anger, continued with his building work.

The people of Watchet, however, were flabbergasted, and quite rightly ashamed of themselves. Henceforth they gave St. Decuman every assistance in building Watchet's first church.

Watchet's *present* parish church is one of the finest in Somerset and proudly bears St. Decuman's name.

The Holy Well still exists and has never been known to run dry. It can easily be found by walking down the lane by the church gates for say 150 yards, then through a little gate on the right. It nestles there among flowers and shrubs in a tranquil setting.

St. Decuman's Well.

THE FLORENCE WYNDHAM STORY

St. Decuman's Church

In the sixteenth century the picturesque old house at Kentsford, near Watchet (now a farmhouse), was the home of John Wyndham and his young wife Florence. John was the elder son of Sir John Wyndham, of Orchard Wyndham, near Williton.

Florence, too, came from a distinguished family. It was her brother, Nicholas Wadham, who founded Wadham College at Oxford.

Sir John and all the family hoped that Florence would bear sons to carry on the Wyndham name.

It seemed that this was not to be when, in 1559, Florence was taken desperately ill and passed into a coma. The local physician was hurriedly summoned to her bedside. After examining her pale and cold body and detecting no pulse, he told the distraught husband that his young wife was dead.

The interment vault of the Wyndham family inside St. Decuman's Church was made ready for the funeral by the sexton. A little earlier this same man had helped to lift Florence's body into her coffin and had noticed that she still wore her golden wedding ring. What a pity, he thought to himself, that this valuable golden token would remain for ever in a tomb and benefit no-one whilst he poor wretch had barely enough to survive. With these thoughts in mind and after the funeral, the sexton gave way to temptation.

At dead of night he stealthily and guiltily opened the heavy church door and, with the light from a candle lantern, made his way to the Wyndham vault and to Florence's coffin.

9

In a cold sweat of fear he tried, without success, to prise the tight-fitting ring from her finger. Not to be beaten, he then attempted to cut off her finger with his sheath knife.

To his horror, blood started to flow from the jagged cut and Florence's arm slowly started to move. Her eyes opened and she uttered a cry of pain.

It seems incredible, but Florence Wyndham was still alive! Amazingly the rough treatment by the sexton had broken her out of a death-like trance (a condition known in the present-day medical profession as catalepsy).

This was far beyond the comprehension of the wretched sexton, who watched petrified as Florence sat up in her coffin. With a wild yell of terror he rushed out of the church and was never seen again.

Florence, however, eventually realised where she was and, picking up the sexton's discarded lantern and attired only in her burial shroud, she made her way down Snailholt Lane and across the meadows to Kentsford.

The great shock, followed by the joy of her reunion can only be left to the imagination, but the legend ends even more happily—for shortly after Florence had returned from the tomb she gave birth to a son. He also was named John and it is from him that the Wyndham line continues to this day.

A poetic version of this legend follows, written about seventy years ago by the late Rev. Lewis Court.

LADY WYNDHAM'S RETURN

On Watchet town the night had closed
   Down by the Severn strand,
And from the grey embattled tower
The bells had chimed the vesper hour,
   Far echoing o'er the land.

Saint Decuman's upon the hill
   kept ward above the town,
And through the silence of the night
The stars like lamps of silver bright
   Their magic rays flashed down.

Kentsford, Somerset

The vale that slept below the shrine,
  With many an elm tree tall,
A stillness held which nothing broke,
Save where—from Warren's stunted oak—
  An owl its mate did call.

But 'neath the Manor's ancient roof
  By Kentsford's murmuring wave,
The noble house of Wyndham kept
A mournful vigil, and they wept
  As round a new-made grave.

And well indeed they might, for late
  Their fair lady had died:
And in the proud ancestral hall
She slept beneath her snow-white pall
  With the lilies by her side.

She was of gentle lineage born
  And to her lord most dear,
A scion he—of ancient clan,
Who now—a broken-hearted man—
  Long lingered by her bier.

11

He thought him of those golden hours
   When he the maiden wooed,
The wedding morn, the nuptial feast,
The blessing of the ancient priest,
   The chancel where they stood.

Now all had vanished as a dream,
   His fondest hopes were gone.
No more those lovely eyes for him
Would shine; his own with tears grew dim
   There in that desolate dawn.

At length the day of burial came,
   And through the leafy lane
Along by Snailholt's silent bourne
They bore her body that sad morn
   Up to the ancient fane.

And there in a grim and mouldy vault,
   Where many a Wyndham lay,
They left her for the long, long rest,
Her white hands crossed upon her breast,
   And went their homeward way.

Again the gathering shades of night
   The little town obscured:
The old church on the breezy mound
Stood silent in its holy ground,
   Its dim vault well secured.

At hour of midnight not a soul
   In Watchet town kept ward,
And while the simple town folk slept
A stealthy figure slowly crept
   Across the sacred sward.

And down the stone steps to the vault
   With furtive glance he made:
Into the lock his rusty key
He ventured, noiseless as could be,
   And startled, half afraid.

The great door yielded: in went he.
    Awhile alarmed he hid;
Then lit his lantern for the quest.
Seized on the leaden burial chest
    And wrenched away the lid.

For well he knew a wealth of gems
    Those dainty fingers wore;
And one, a ring a ransom worth.
Too rich to moulder in the earth.
    Which she would want no more.

And those were days of dire distress
    For men of low estate:
And glittering gold and sparkling gem
Could have no further use for them
    Whom death had dealt their fate.

With thoughts like these his wavering will
    The guilty sexton steeled.
And resolute followed yet the quest
Till, flashing from that peaceful breast.
    The gems were clear revealed.

He seized the slender fingers white
    And stiff in their repose.
Then sought to file the circlet through;
When, to his horror, blood he drew.
    And the fair sleeper rose.

She sat a moment, gazed around.
    Then, great was her surprise.
And sexton, startled, saw at a glance
This was not death, but a deep trance.
    And madness leapt to his eyes.

The stagnant life stream in her veins
    Again began to flow:
She felt the sudden quickening.
For her it was a joyous thing.
    For him a fearsome woe.

He sprang, and like a madman fled
　　From the accusing vault,
And made his way among the tombs
As one chased by a hundred dooms,
　　Who dared not call a halt.

The lady beckoned him in vain,
　　He was too scared to heed.
She would have given him his price;
He cleared the churchyard in a trice,
　　Spurred by his desperate deed.

And never came he back again,
　　Nor could the people tell
His whereabout; but legend tells
He followed the pathway up Five Bells
　　And leapt into a well.

The lady Wyndham left her bier,
　　And by the lantern's aid
She scaled the damp stone steps and found
Her way across the holy ground
　　And straightway homeward made.

All down by Snailholt's silent meads
　　The ghostly figure passed,
And through the list'ning grove below:
The startled kine that watched her go
　　Sprang up with fear aghast.

She reached the Manor lawn at length,
　　Paused at the porchway hatch;
And then, as one held in a dream,
Her face as pale in the lantern's beam,
　　She lifted clear the latch.

But bolts and bars were safely set:
　　She gave a gentle knock;
Then louder; and at length she heard
A sound, as though someone had stirred,
　　And it was one o' the clock.

Now sleep that lonesome night forsook
  The sorrowing husband there:
He heard the river murmuring by,
And marked the mute stars in the sky
  That seemed to mock his prayer.

Hour after hour he wakeful lay
  And all disconsolate,
When, suddenly, he heard a sound,
Then the baying of his faithful hound
  And the click of the court-house gate.

Then knockings at the great hall door
  And a most plaintiff call:
He rose and oped the casement wide,
And through the darkness he descried
  A ghostly figure tall.

The lantern in her hand she held,
  Her robe was spectral white:
Here surely one had come from the dead!
His heart it thumped with a great dread:
  It was an awesome sight.

What wonder such a vision made
  His knees together knock!
Yet fear should not his soul unman,
So down the oaken stairs he ran
  And seized his old flint-lock.

Some rustic knave or fool, thought he,
  Is playing me this prank:
And if he is not soon away
Begad! I'll make short work of his play;
  Yet half in fear he shrank.

He threw the parvise casement wide
  And rang the challenge down,
"Who art thou? Answer, or I'll shoot!"
The figure stood a moment mute,
  And fearful of his frown.

Kentsford, the home of Florence Wyndham.

Then eagerly she made reply,
    "Shoot not! I am you wife.
Come down, I pray you, let me in!
For the night is chill and my garb is thin,
    And God gives me back my life."

The voice was hers beyond all doubt:
    His wife it was who spake,
Ah! That the dead should come again
To haunt the ways of troubled men
    And other troubles make.

"Death held me not: it was a trance,"
    She cried. "Oh, tarry not!
This winding sheet about my breast
Yet wears the embroidered Wyndham crest:
    Pity my helpless lot."

He bounded down the great hall stairs
  And opened wide the door:
Clasping her in a fond embrace,
He wiped the tears from that sweet face
  He had thought to see no more.

She told him all the ghostly tale
  Of the vault, the sexton's flight,
The file that made her finger bleed,
The venture down the lonesome mead,
  The grim and terrible night.

So there was joy that early dawn
  in the Squire of Kentsford's hall,
Joy as of hearts all newly wed
For one who has risen from the dead
  To bear him sons withal.

And sons she after bore him, twain,
  To keep the Wyndham name:
And many a year she lived to grace
His board and hearth, and all the place
  Resounded with her fame.

And still in old St. Decuman's
  The tablet may be seen,
Which bears the name of the lady fair
And her two children sculptured there,
  To keep her memory green.

Lewis H. Court, Exon.

FOR THOSE IN PERIL

From storm and tempest, fire and foe—
Protect us where so ere we go.

So run the words of a well-known hymn.

For hundreds of years Watchet has endured and survived all the perils mentioned and indeed has had more than its share of storms.

Situated on a very exposed part of the coast, the harbour and town and the soft red cliffs have constantly been eroded away by the angry sea.

During the sixteenth century disastrous storms washed away large parts of Watchet and the nearby hamlet of Doniford.

At that time local people were quite dismayed by the words of an elderly lady visitor from Yorkshire. This person was quite notorious and known nationwide as OLD MOTHER SHIPTON. She was a soothsayer and a prophetess of doom. Many people believed she was a witch.

After seeing and hearing of the constant erosion, the mischievous old lady, in a cackling and hag-like voice, recited the following ominous rhyme:

Watchet and Doniford both shall drown,
And Williton become the seaport town.

Shortly after making this alarming prophesy, old Mother Shipton died and is said to be buried in a wood at Williton (two miles inland from Watchet).

A headstone with mysterious insignia marks the very place, but some sceptical people believe the stone to be hoax erected there in the eighteenth century.

Be that as it may, the residents of Watchet and Doniford cannot say they have not been warned, and it may be as well for them to keep their hymn books handy.

THE COMBE SYDENHAM LEGEND

A very interesting old house and estate is situated near Monksilver — about three miles from Watchet.

Known originally as 'Combe' it was held in 1086 by William de Mohun. Late in the fourteenth century and for over three hundred years it was owned by the Sydenhams — hence its name — Combe Sydenham. Later it was the home of the Notley family.

Today the historic old house and its grounds, owned by W. A. C. Theed, Esq., is open to the public and much enjoyed by visitors.

There is a captivating 16th century legend featuring Sir George Sydenham's daughter, Elizabeth. Seemingly she was very much in love and engaged to marry Sir Francis Drake, the famous circumnavigator of the world. They planned to marry as soon as he returned from his next foray against the Spanish fleet.

Sir George had never really taken to Drake and would have preferred his daughter to marry an interested local wealthy man.

After several years had passed, Drake had not returned from his travels. Sir George, therefore, persuaded Elizabeth that Drake was unlikely ever to return and in all probability was dead. She should, he insisted, marry the local affluent suitor.

After much parental pressure Elizabeth reluctantly agreed.

On the set wedding day, fortunately just before she had taken her wedding vows, there was a terrific bang, a blinding flash and a 'cannon ball' hurtled down from the sky. "Gadzooks, what the devil was that?" cried Sir George in great alarm.

"Methinks it's a signal from my Francis", said Elizabeth quite calmly, and she refused point blank to proceed with the wedding. Her intuition was quite right. Drake had returned to Plymouth that very day and he hastened to claim his bride.

It is recorded that they were married in 1585.

As for the cannon ball, it is still there for all to see. There are some people who claim it is a meteorite and not a cannon ball at all.

Be that as it may, it did the trick and the local wealthy man, although quite upset, had no difficulty in finding another bride.

GEORGE ESKOTT AND THE PIRATE

Throughout history pirates have been the bane of sailors and ship-owners. They infested every ocean and were not unknown even in the Bristol Channel.

In 1610, during the reign of King James I, a pirate by the name of Thomas Salkeld, with a band of cut-throats, set up a stronghold on Lundy Island in mid-channel. From this base they attacked and captured unsuspecting merchant ships which occasionally sought shelter in the lee of the island. The ships' crews, if not murdered, were taken against their will onto the island where Salkeld lived like an emperor, supported by his gang of rogues.

The captured sailors were made to work like slaves and had to live like animals in cowsheds at one end of the island. They might well have been prisoners for life had it not been for George Eskott, a Watchet mariner.

George's ship, before it too was captured by Salkeld, had been bound for Bridgwater with a cargo which included casks of brandy. Forced ashore at swordpoint, George and his crew joined other captured sailors who were very unhappy at their predicament. They said they had often considered rebellion but, being unarmed, they feared the result.

George was determined he would not submit to slavery, but wisely decided to bide his time. He suspected that before long Salkeld and his louts would be drinking the brandy from his ship, which was still at anchor, and he knew, from experience, that it was very potent indeed. Sure enough, later that very night the pirates brought ashore and broached a large cask of brandy. Soon after they were heard singing and laughing uproariously. Some of the captives wanted to mount an attack at once but George held them back. "Hang about," he said, "let them have a bellyful first." This was sound advice for a couple of hours later the pirates were "three sheets in the wind" and seen staggering about. "Now's our chance, my hearties, follow me," cried George, and picking up a shovel, he led the way across the island to Salkeld's grand mansion.

With a mighty swipe of his shovel, George floored a huge bearded pirate guarding the entrance who was 'as drunk as a hand-cart'. Closely followed by his comrades, George then charged into the pirates' lair. As he had expected, the scoundrels were all 'gunnels under' and no match for him and his sober sailors.

Only Salkeld drew his cutlass and stood up unsteadily to fight. George advanced, calling on him in the name of King James to surrender. The pirate replied by lashing out viciously with his sword. George parried the attack with his trusty shovel, then quick as a flash struck back, breaking the tyrant's arm. Salkeld screamed with pain and rage.

It was all over—the pirates were trussed up with spun yarn and the next day were transported aboard George's ship to the mainland. Handed over to the authorities, they were hanged by their necks until they were dead.

In due course the news of Salkeld's capture and his fate was brought to the notice of King James. The King wrote thanking George for doing his duty. What is more, he awarded George Eskott of Watchet a pension of eighteen pence a day—no mean sum in those days.

The Pirate.

PART II —
OLD WATCHET CUSTOMS

WATCHET COURT LEET

For hundreds of years and even into the early nineteenth century, the entire civic administration and the law and order of Watchet was the responsibility of Watchet Court Leet. This organisation was not unique, for similar bodies existed in towns and villages throughout the country. They were the recognised authorities where all matters of local importance were settled.

Here at Watchet from time immemorial the Court Leet meetings were held at the Bell Inn in Market Street. All the main sessions were presided over by the Steward of the Wyndham Estate—delegated by the Lord of the Manor.

Another most important officer was the Port Reeve. He was one of a number of Watchet landowners and as such had no option but to take his turn as Port Reeve for a year's duration. His duties involved the tedious task of collecting all fines and tolls as well as ground rents on certain properties, and landing dues on cargoes of coal, salt and flour. From the monies thus collected he paid all the expenses of the Court and kept proper account. Any surplus money was invested for future Court Leet contingencies.

Other officers and workmen appointed by the Court Leet included an Inspector of Weights and Measures; an Inspector of Nuisances; a Foreman of the Jury; a Stock Driver; a Town Crier; an Ale Taster; two Constables; two Scavengers; and a Pig Driver.

With the possible exception of the Ale Taster, it is unlikely any of the men volunteered for their jobs. They were, however, summoned to present themselves at court by the Bailiff, and warned that failure to attend would be *'at their peril'*. In addition to his appointed job, each man had to serve on the jury whenever wrongdoers were brought before the court. So it was that countless generations of Court Leet officials were pressed into service to ensure the smooth running of the town.

They did, however, enjoy one much envied perk, for after the business of the main October session they all sat down to a sumptuous dinner which included roast goose and a noggin of hot punch, all paid for by the Port Reeve.

It is quite possible that the origin of the Watchet Court Leet goes back a thousand years, for Watchet was a 'defended town' in the tenth century and the site of a Royal Mint. In 1243 Watchet was known as a borough and in 1302 was requested to send two members to Parliament.

Watchet Court Leet at the Bell Inn. 1948. Left to right: J. Stephens, H. J. Norman. H. Short. J. H. Norman, E. Nicholas, E. Shorney. J. Pittaway, H. Redd (Bailiff). A. T. Love (President), A. Short. W. J. Lee, T. B. Peel. A. Allen, Dr. Collins.

23

The earliest Court records, however, start in 1273 when cases of trespass and debt were dealt with.

In 1471 three Watchet men were brought to court after having set upon one 'Henry Irishman' with a sword, a bill-hook and a dagger. One of them, Robert Grey, was fined twelve pence for making 'a great noise and disturbing the court'.

Many matters dealt with by the court at that time concerned straying animals, some of which were impounded and their owners fined. Public rights of way were kept under constant review and no obstruction tolerated.

Roads as we know them today did not exist but rough tracks, if very soggy, were ballasted with stones or shingle by the court.

In 1473, Govier's Lane, a sunken track leading directly inland from the harbour, was reported as needing such repair. It had gradually been worn deeper and deeper by the hooves of countless packhorses. Apart from oxen-drawn sledges this was the usual way of transporting goods to and from the harbour.

In 1629 Elizabeth Haringe was fined for 'harking' at night, at the door of her neighbour, and in 1711 a disgusting fellow by the name of John Perrett was reported for emptying his chamber pot into the street. In 1773 it was reported that the Court Leet Pillory and its ducking stool needed repairs and so were not available for correcting nagging women or witches.

In 1820 Williams, a butcher from Monksilver, was fined five shillings for using faulty steelyards to weigh some meat at Watchet.

These are just a few samples from the records, but give an idea of the varied matters dealt with by the court and although they may seem amusing to us today, they were in their time considered to be serious offences.

When necessary, persons suspected of more serious crimes were held temporarily in a small lock-up cell whilst awaiting trial. If committed to prison they were taken to Taunton gaol by the Court Leet's own constables, assisted if required by hired guardsmen.

Gradually, from about 1830, District and County Councils and Regional Police Authorities took over the functions of all Court Leets throughout the country. Consequently the majority of these bodies disbanded or just faded away.

Fortunately this did not happen at Watchet where people recognised the Court Leet to be a colourful link with the town's historical past. The Court Leet, therefore, was not disbanded and, in fact, its authority has never been officially rescinded.

Encouraged by the Wyndham family, the court continues to meet annually and ceremoniously. The venue, however, has changed in recent years and the annual October meeting currently takes place at the

Downfield Hotel.

Here, as ordered by the bailiff, proceedings start at "TWELVE O'CLOCK IN THE FORENOON PRECISELY". Outside the hotel the town crier, in full regalia, will have announced to all and sundry that the Court Leet 'has assembled within'.

Dead on time, the Bailiff taps the floor sharply with his six-foot staff of office and loudly declares: "THE COURT LEET IS NOW IN SESSION".

After being handed a copy of the precept, the President proclaims: "ALL PERSONS WHO OWE SUIT AND SERVICE AT THE COURT LEET AND COURT BARON NOW TO BE HOLDEN FOR THE TOWN AND BOROUGH OF WATCHET, DRAW NEAR AND ANSWER TO YOUR NAMES'.

The Bailiff, after calling the names, disapprovingly marks absent any-one who after being called three times fails to answer. (Absentees face heavy fines.)

The Foreman of the Jury is then sworn by the President "TO KEEP THE QUEEN'S COUNCIL, TO PRESENT NOTHING OUT OF HATRED OR MALICE, AND TO CONCEAL NOTHING OUT OF FEAR, FAVOUR OR AFFECTION, SO HELP HIM GOD". All other jurors summoned to attend are similarly sworn and kiss the Bible.

Then comes the allocation of the traditional Court Leet 'jobs' (ale-taster, scavenger, etc.). Nowadays it is unlikely that these officers will be overworked, except perhaps the Town Crier. He is often called upon to attend at functions and to announce forthcoming events.

As has been the custom for hundreds of years, the court's official busi-ness is followed by the customary dinner of roast goose, apple-pie with clotted cream, and walnuts. Then comes a goodly goblet or two of piping hot punch—the secret recipe for which has been handed down from ages past. Without fail glasses are raised to toast Her Majesty the Queen, and again to the Wyndham family and the President.

During the year 1988, Watchet celebrated its millennium. Many his-toric events of the past thousand years were re-enacted, including an invasion of the port by Viking longboats. To play its part in the pro-gramme of events known as "WATCHET 1,000" the Court Leet con-vened a special open-air session on the Esplanade. A person (obviously a witch) was spotted amongst the large crowd of spectators and brought 'before the court'. After a fair trial the person was found to be guilty and the ancient ducking stool was once more put to good use. It was all great fun and the 'rough justice' was much enjoyed by thousands of people (as well as the victim).

The old Court Leet lock-up in Market Street has recently been res-tored by the Watchet Museum Society. The iron grille on its door pro-vides a further reminder of Watchet's historic past. With the adjoining

Watchet Court Leet Lock-up.

Jessie Norman's pitiful cries of innocence ignored by the Court Leet officials.
Photo by R. Priddy

museum and the on-going Court Leet it is part of the town's heritage.

HOT CAKES AND CIDER

One of Watchet's earliest industries was the weaving of woollen cloth. During the seventeenth century packs of this commodity were regularly shipped away. Some of the finished cloth was known as WATCHET BLUE and is thought to have been dyed that colour with the juice of locally-picked whortleberries.

It is recorded that in 1553 some Watchet Blue cloth was used to make sailors' uniforms for an ill-fated expedition to China which was led by Sir Hugh Willoughby, and that in 1649 King Charles I wore a waistcoat of WATCHET BLUE as he walked to the scaffold.

Some years later a Queen Catherine—believed to be the wife of King Charles II—visited Watchet to select for herself some lengths of the celebrated material. Now this Queen Catherine was a Portuguese lady and her visit to Watchet was in late November. Could it be possible that being susceptible to the cold she desired to have a warm woollen cloak made, or maybe some Watchet Blue pantaloons. Alas, we shall never know!

Catherine of Braganza, Queen Consort of Charles II.

By all account Queen Catherine (or Caturn as she was known to Watchet folk) was well pleased with her royal welcome and before she left the town she generously provided a feast for everyone of HOT CAKES AND CIDER. The treat was so enjoyed that the townsfolk decided to make it an annual event. Every year, therefore, on 23rd November folk would gather in the evening in little groups to partake of a similar feast. It was known as Caturn's Night.

After tucking into their hot cakes, helped down by noggins of cider, they would happily look forward to their next festive occasion at Christmas. With this in mind, they would altogether recite the following jingle:

> 'Tis Caturn's Night we do believe
> And tomorrow month be Christmas Eve.
> Hurrah. Hurrah. Hurrah!

Celebrations of Caturn's Night are now quite rare, but before the days of radio and TV these simple mid-winter get-togethers were greatly enjoyed. All thanks to good Queen Caturn.

ST. DECUMAN'S FAIR

For centuries St. Decuman's Fair (known sometimes as Watchet Fair) was held each September in Market Street. It was an annual three-day event—sadly now beyond living memory.

All manner of goods were for sale on open stalls and the people of the town thronged the narrow street eager for bargains. It was a colourful scene, with musicians, buskers, folk dancers, etc. The activities increased after dark, swelled by many folk after their daily work. The whole street was lit by flares and candles for it was before the time of street lighting.

One old gentleman who could remember the fair was the late Captain Tom Allen, who told the writer of the following incident:

As a boy, Captain Tom and another lad were on their way one evening to the fair each with a candle lantern. Ahead of them in narrow Govier's Lane a man was walking slowly and apparently leading a large dog. The animal seemed to be shuffling along in a strange manner and, as they nervously passed by, the creature reared up on its hind legs to a height of near seven feet and growled. The poor lads fled in terror.

Later that night at the fair they saw the same man playing a flute and a large bear on its hind legs dancing to the music.

LANTERN NIGHT

A simple little annual event much enjoyed by children years ago was known as LANTERN NIGHT. It took place as soon as it was dark on September 16th and was a surviving reminder of WATCHET FAIR.

Many groups of children, including toddlers, would wander around the town each carrying a candle lantern. Most of these had been painstakingly made by the children themselves by hollowing out a mangold or swede. Some were quite artistic and others carved to resemble a grotesque human face.

To the children of today Lantern Night activities might appear uninteresting and 'corny', but to youngsters years ago to venture out into the dark carrying their own flickering lantern was an exciting adventure, and to the little ones—pure magic!

During the Second World War a complete blackout was ordered and no exterior light permitted. Consequently the traditional Lantern Night walk-about was brought to a close.

The end of this old Watchet custom was probably not regretted by the local farmers who, from time immemorial, had tolerated the disappearance of hundredweights of root crops—all having been carried off from their fields by the youngsters.

PUTTING UP THE BROOM

No-one knows when the quaint old Watchet custom of PUTTING UP THE BROOM started. Its origin is a mystery shrouded in the mists of time. Nevertheless, in olden days it was generally known in the town that a broom—prominently displayed outside a house—was a sign indicating to passers-by that a lady housekeeper or home help was required within.

According to old folk this simple method of advertising for domestic help was brought into disrepute around the end of the nineteenth century, mainly by young pranksters out for mischief at night. Consequently at this time any husband whose wife was away from home for a night or so might awaken to find that without his knowledge a broom had been fastened conspicuously high up, or even to the chimney pot of his house. It was all very embarrassing. Passers-by would be tittering and, although no real harm was done, not every victim was amused.

Sometimes the mischievous lads would go too far and add a crude notice such as "Half a bed to let". Even elderly and confirmed bachelors who lived alone were liable to find a broom and saucy notice displayed. The situation at that time was becoming out of hand.

Well-known Watchet journalist Will Lee still at his desk on his 82nd birthday in 1950.

The late Mr. Willie Lee, a well-known Watchet journalist, told the writer that he himself, when but a lad, had misguidedly(?) taken part in one of the last of these pranks. "Unfortunately," he said, "it went wrong." He and his friend, Arthur Balmer, had been told (with a nudge and a wink) that Mr. Walter Foy's wife was away from home visiting relatives. With several other youths they waited until after midnight and the gas street lights had been extinguished. A long ladder — owned by the Parish Council and kept for fire emergencies behind the Market House—was 'borrowed' and quietly set up against Mr. Foy's jeweller's shop and room above in Swain Street. Arthur Balmer, with a broom and a piece of rope in his hand, had just climbed onto the roof when Mr. Foy stepped out of his shop. Everyone fled—except poor Arthur, who was left stranded on the roof. Mr. Foy having moved the ladder, Arthur had no option but to remain there until his pitiable cries for help were heard by people in the adjoining houses. Eventually Mr. Foy relented and the ladder was put back in place.

This was not the end of the matter, for according to Mr. Lee the escapade came to the notice of the pastors of the Baptist and Wesleyan Churches. "It caused great consternation," he said, and the following Sunday the practice was denounced from both pulpits as offensive and wholly unacceptable.

GLATTING

An unusual custom, possibly unique to the Watchet and West Somerset seashore, was that of hunting conger eels with dogs.

This age-old practice known as GLATTING was, in its way, similar to the countryman's sport of "rabbiting". In years past the writer has participated in both of these local activities which in the hard times pre-war provided 'something for the pot'!

Whereas rabbits would usually be found in burrows in hedgerows, conger eels could be located in cavities under rocky ledges exposed by the ebb tide. In each case a trained dog could sniff out and indicate in its own excited manner where a rabbit or conger eel was hidden from view.

To bolt a rabbit from its burrow a ferret would be used, but a conger eel would have to be prodded vigorously with an eight or ten-foot ash or hazel stick before it would rush out of its holt. The conger's abode was often hidden by seaweed and situated at the side of a shallow pond.

To see a dog tackling a thrashing conger in the water is now a rare sight indeed, but fifty years ago it was quite common. The eels some-

Local fisherman Clifford Beaver with two of his conger-hunting dogs and a 27lb. conger.

Mr. Beaver prodding for a conger in its holt.

times measured six feet in length and could weigh up to thirty pounds, but on average they weighed about six or seven pounds. They were not killed by the dogs but by a quick blow on the head with a hook-shaped iron bar known as a GLATHOOK. Often the eels would evade capture when, after a skirmish, the water in the pond muddied and they could not again be found.

All along the seashore from Stolford and Kilve to Watchet and Blue Anchor, conger hunters would wait for the ebb of the biggest spring tides which allowed them access to the hunting grounds. The dogs were of no particular breed, but among them were quite a few veterans who bore scars of battle, including "Rex", a three-legged lurcher at Watchet.

PART III — ANECDOTES

ONE OF GOD'S CREATURES

In the 1930s, with several other lads, I was told this rather gruesome tale about a cat by a fisherman whose name was Fred. (Anyone of a squeamish disposition—be warned—do not read on!)

Fred and his wife had taken up residence in a cottage near the harbour. The former occupants of the cottage owned an elderly black cat and, although they had taken it with them when they moved, it returned time after time to its old home and tried to settle down as before.

Fred did not take kindly to the cat as it was not an affectionate and lovable creature. "It would never purr," he said, "and what is more it had nasty habits." He made many efforts to shoo it away by shouting and hissing and waving his arms about. All to no avail. The artful creature would 'bide its time' and then creep back into the house. In despair, Fred sought advice from an old friend who was knowledgeable in the ways of cats. His friend considered the cat would never mend its ways and suggested that Fred should borrow his Jack Russell terrier for a few days. The cat, he said, would then run far away and never return. Fred mused doubtfully on this suggestion and rather unwisely mentioned it to his wife, who loved cats. She was furious. "How dare you ever think of such a thing," she cried, "the poor dear cat is one of God's creatures and put on this earth for a purpose. Don't you ever lay a finger on that poor dear animal!"

Being all for a quiet life, Fred immediately agreed not to harm the cat in any way. However, a few days later while his wife was out shopping the cat had again misbehaved. "One of God's creatures it might be," he muttered to himself, "but I'm the one who always has to attend to the nasty work." Feeling very aggrieved, he noticed the cat slinking out through the partly open door and he groped around quickly in a cupboard for his slipper—his intention being to fling the slipper in protest at the fast disappearing culprit. Unfortunately in his hurry he picked up and flung his boot—which was of the hobnail variety. The poor cat was struck on the head and immediately dropped dead.

Fred recoiled in horror for he had not intended to harm the cat; his only intention was to frighten it away. He was full of remorse and sorrow, and fearful of his wife's reaction. He decided to hide the body (and later dispose of it) and meanwhile to say nothing to his wife. So—after putting the corpse in a cardboard box—he hid it behind a bush in the garden.

Later that night, having told his wife he had to go to the harbour to attend to his boat. he picked up the box and set off, feeling very ill at ease. It was a dark and dirty night and it seemed to him that there were more cats around than normal. He could hear them wailing eerily and occasionally he caught sight of one and imagined it was looking at him accusingly with its glowing eyes.

Arriving at the harbour he threw the box as far as he could into the darkness and heard it splash into the water. He knew that the ebbing tide and offshore wind would carry the box far out to sea where it would sink and he hoped that that would be the end of the matter. Feeling like a guilty murderer, he walked slowly homewards. Glumly he wondered if there might be an after-life for cats—a cats' heaven perhaps, with cat-like angels flying from cloud to cloud.

Passing a flickering gas-lamp, his heart missed a beat for he felt almost certain he'd glimpsed a black feline shadow streak past. Was it, he wondered fearfully, a phantom cat sent to haunt and torment him?

Imagine Fred's shock, therefore, when he arrived home and found a black cat sitting on the doorstep. It was identical to the one he'd just thrown into the harbour AND WAS DRIPPING WET. Almost at once the truth dawned on him, for it was indeed the same cat. Apparently it had not died when struck by the boot but had passed into an unconscious state. The cold ducking in the harbour, Fred explained, had shocked and revived the cat. It had then courageously struck out for the landing steps and bolted home—passing him on the way.

Fred was so relieved that he took the poor bedraggled animal into the house and dried it in front of the fire. "Some cruel boys must have thrown a bucket of water over this poor creature," he suggested to his wife, who was most concerned at its pitiful state. Fred then gave it half of a herring that he had intended having for his supper.

Henceforth the cat was allowed into the house and lived happily for several years. It learned how to purr and, according to Fred, from that time onwards was completely cured of its nasty habits.

HEARTS OF OAK

During the latter part of the nineteenth century iron ore was extensively mined on the Brendon Hills. Thousands of tons were transported from the mines to Watchet Harbour on the specially built West Somerset Mineral Railway. It was then shipped across the Bristol Channel to be smelted in the Iron Works at Ebbw Vale. Although busy for many years, the mining industry was eventually unable to compete with cheaper iron ore imported from Spain. By 1910 all mining had ceased and the mines and the Mineral Railway lay derelict.

An amusing and possibly 'tongue in cheek' anecdote concerning the end of the railway was related to the writer many years ago. The storyteller was Bert Bale—a Watchet mariner and notorious spinner of yarns. He explained that during the 1914-18 war there was a national shortage of iron and steel, and the Ministry of Munitions ordered that the steel rails of the disused railway should be taken up for use elsewhere. Mr. Tom Peel, a well-known local yachtsman and business man, was placed in charge of the operation. At that time there was a shortage of labour—most young men had been called up. Tom, therefore, engaged sailors (including Bert) who were ashore at Watchet awaiting a ship. The work entailed travelling some six miles to the end of the mineral line at Comberow, disconnecting the rails and loading them onto railway trucks. The trucks were then hauled by horsepower to Watchet Harbour—the rails unloaded and later shipped away. The sailors could either walk to work or make use of an old track maintenance trolley which could be propelled along by manually pumping handles up and down. This was quite hard work but considered better than walking, especially on the return journey which was, in places, slightly downhill and therefore required less pumping.

Bert recalled that on one breezy day Georgie Strong (one of the sailors) turned up for work carrying a boat's mast and lug sail. He suggested setting the sail on the trolley as the wind was fresh from the north-east and blowing in the right direction. Tom Peel was consulted and readily agreed. He loved a bit of fun and so he popped home for a naval officer's hat which he always wore when he went sailing and he let everyone know that he was taking command. While the mast and sail were being rigged the trolley was made fast to the track, and about a hundred townsfolk gathered to see the 'ship on wheels' set sail. As a safety precaution to give warning to anyone walking on the track, a hand-operated bellows type foghorn was borrowed from a schooner lying alongside the west pier, and one 'Tuncle' Harris (the only non-sailor employed by Tom) was instructed 'how to operate it'. Eventually all eight members of the crew (including the landlubber Harris) climbed aboard. Looking quite smart in his officer's hat, Tom inspected

Mr. Thomas Barton Peel, well-known Watchet character and sportsman.

his men, then, after appointing Bert as first mate, he crisply gave the order 'cast off for'ard, let go aft'.

The wind was quite strong and the trolley with its sail hoisted was straining at its moorings. Bosun Binding was bending over the stern endeavouring to release the mooring rope. He was suddenly tugged head first over the side as the trolley unexpectedly shot forward under full sail. "Man overboard," cried Tom, but the trolley gathered way and Bosun Binding was left behind frantically waving his arms and uttering words which were quite offensive and cannot be recorded here. Although comparatively unhurt, Bosun was embarrassed and annoyed by the tittering and smirking of the onlookers. He was especially irked by the antics of two old hobblers who were rolling helplessly about gasping for breath and laughing their fool heads off.

Meanwhile, according to Bert, things were none too happy aboard the trolley. It forged ahead and passed Whitehall Cottages at a hair-raising pace with the fog-horn going full blast. As they surged past the paper mill Bert estimated their speed to be at least 20 knots! However, his suggestion to Tom to put a reef in the sail was rejected out of hand. "Have no fear, my boy, don't panic, and always remember that fortune favours the brave," replied Tom, with a smile stretching from ear to ear. He loved speed and was in his element. (Secretly he was hoping to improve on and claim the Watchet to Comberow speed record held until then by the veteran steam locomotive Pontypool). His eyes were gleaming with excitement and Bert felt sure that had there been a square sail or a spinnaker aboard, Tom would have hoisted it in addition to the billowing lugsail. Georgie Strong, who was grimly holding on with both hands, felt very uneasy at the trolley's amazing turn of speed. He regretted having suggested the idea in the first place. Turning to fisherman Sammy Hake, who was as white as a sheet and feeling landsick, he querulously asked "Where be it all going to end?"

Farmer Shorney at nearby Kentsford Farm was quietly enjoying his breakfast. On hearing the mournful notes of the foghorn he rushed out in alarm thinking that one of his cows was about to give birth. He could hardly believe his eyes when he saw the trolley speeding by. "You'll never believe it," he explained to his wife, "there was Tom Peel sailing along the line, going like billy-oh ee was and laughing fit to bust."

In the meantime the 'Comberow Clipper" with its colourful crew continued its remarkable voyage. When Bye Farm loomed up on the starboard bow, Tom did his best to raise the morale of his men. In what Bert described as 'a rich baritone voice', he sang a Royal Navy ditty entitled HEARTS OF OAK. This he delivered with great spirit and patriotic fervour, and the sailors, having by this time got over their jitters, joined heartily in the chorus. STEADY, BOYS, STEADY they sang in delightful harmony. The only one not singing was Cape Horn veteran 'Windy' Allen. Peeved at not being appointed first mate, 'Windy' sat sulking on the poop deck and sullenly smoking a foul-smelling pipe. His reputation of sailing through the Roaring Forties had been disregarded and he felt slighted. He further demonstrated his resentment by noisily hawking and spitting at the end of each verse.

The wind continued blowing quite strongly as the songsters sailed blissfully through the countryside. Little did they realise what a nautical nightmare lay ahead. So engrossed were they in their singing that they completely forgot the level crossing at Washford which was across the line.

As soon as the gates came in view Tom urgently barked out the order, "Lower the mainsail and apply full brakes." Unfortunately this was not immediately possible as the halliards had become twisted and the main sheet could not be released as it had somehow got tangled around Tuncle Harris's foot. Although the brakes were frantically applied, they pro-

ved quite incapable of arresting the careering truck under the pressure of its billowing lugsail. Pulled with excessive force by able seaman Walty Norman, the rusty brake lever broke off in his hand. "Oh my God, now us be done for," wailed Sammy Hake. "Lord 'elp us, we be all doomed," groaned Georgie Strong. The collision with the gates was inevitable. The 'Comberow Clipper' took a violent list to port and was thrown onto its beam ends. Everyone aboard was hurled into a heap and regrettably panic set in among the lower ranks. "Abandon ship," gasped Tom, but his voice now lacked its usual clarity. He and 'Windy' Allen (who had broken his pipe) were both hopping mad. All the others were battered and bruised and each in turn castigated the unfortunate landlubber Harris. His awkwardness and lack of seamanship, they declared, was the cause of the shipwreck.

Whether the sailors carried on walking to work or whether they packed up for the day, Bert did not make clear when relating this tale. He did, however, say that 'after the dust had settled', Tuncle Harris was in tears and he saw Georgie Strong ruefully looking at the broken mast (borrowed by him from John Besley's fishing boat) and heard him sadly muttering . . . "We could 'ave stopped if only we'd brought the blasted anchor!"

THE BULL RUN

All the dogs would be barking. Men and boys would be shouting, "LOOK OUT. LOOK OUT. HERE THEY COME". Everyone walking or standing in Watchet's narrow Swain Street, on hearing the commotion, would dive for cover and safety into the nearest shop and shut the door. They would have to be quick for down the street would come thundering four or five wild-looking bullocks driven pell-mell by Tom Gregory and Howard Strong.

Butcher boy Henry Binding, having cycled on in advance to warn people, would bravely stand in the middle of the street near the Post Office. With Albert Phillips, he would divert the snorting, galloping beasts into Esplanade Lane. Here, the long-established butcher, Thomas Hooper, would be waiting to turn them into his yard and eventually to his slaughterhouse.

Exciting mini bull-runs such as this would take place every week prior to World War II when Watchet's meat supply was delivered "on the hoof". However, the runs didn't always pass off without incident as, according to butcher Hooper's daughter Mary, a bullock once charged into Mr. W. G. Penny's tailor's shop and played havoc. "W.G." (as Mr. Penny was familiarly known) was a great local character and sportsman. He drove the frenzied creature out of the shop and down the street with his cricket bat!

W. G. Penny, of Watchet, for 13 seasons secretary to the St. Decuman's C.C.

THE EXPERT

From ages back and certainly until the 1950s quite a few townsfolk kept a pig at the end of their gardens for their own consumption. The pigs were fed on kitchen waste and surplus garden produce, all of which was boiled and then mixed with barley meal or bran.

When their pig was ready for killing, some owners would call on the services of the local 'pig expert' known as 'Crafty'. For a modest sum 'Crafty' would kill, scald and scrape, and cut up the pig on the owner's premises. If requested, he would help to 'salt in' the meat and deal with the chitterlings.

One of the funniest pig-moving episodes witnessed by Howard Strong was when 'Bowler Hat Billy' drove an enormous pig from his yard at the rear of Swain Street en route to butcher Hooper's slaughterhouse. With great difficulty he had 'walked it' as far as Mr. Wally West's shop when it sat down and refused to budge. Billy, having handled pigs before, knew that a bucket placed over a pig's head could make it walk backwards to get its head out of the bucket. Borrowing a galvanised pail from Mr. West, he approached the huge pig head-on. Unfortunately Billy was quite short and also bow-legged, and the artful pig, spotting daylight between Billy's legs, put its head down and charged. The bucket went flying, and Billy found himself sitting astride the pig and facing backwards as it careered up the street. Bert Hunt in the Saskatoon Cafe was heard shouting, "Ride him, cowboy!" but Billy could hold on no longer and was thrown off head first by the galloping porker.

Fortunately, Billy was saved from serious injury by his bowler hat, which, however, was badly battered and dented. There were other pig owners as well as Billy who drove their own animals to the slaughterhouse of other butchers in the town. Their efforts, too, were often hilarious, for pigs are the most obstinate of creatures and will move only in the opposite direction to the one desired! Spectators seemed to appear from nowhere to see the fun and occasionally the frustrated pig-owners would abandon the task and, in desperation, call for 'Crafty'.

'Crafty' always knew how to deal with the situation. He was after all THE EXPERT.

THE KNOWLEDGE

Until water supplies were nationalised by the Government in 1973, many towns and villages were supplied with water by their local council authorities or by private companies. Some of these companies were quite big—others quite small, as was the Watchet Water Company.

44

From the year 1889 this private company supplied the town with water from springs in the Brendon Hills. The water was piped to a reservoir at 'Parsonage'—200 feet above the town. From there it gravitated in cast iron pipes to the streets and houses below.

The only staff employed by the company was a secretary, who also collected the water rates (a tiny fraction of what they are today). All maintenance and repairs to the system were carried out by a local plumber who had an agreement to give priority to the company's work.

After a fire in the secretary's office in the 1920s, no plans whatever survived to show the position of the company's mains, sluice valves, hydrants and stopcocks. The whereabouts of all these essential points were stored only in the head of the current plumber who would have 'served his time' with the previous plumber. He was, therefore, *the man with the KNOWLEDGE* and was often referred to as such by the company directors.

By and large, all went well under this system until the Second World War. Things then started to go wrong. First the plumber's apprentice was called up to serve in the Armed Forces. Then, all within a short period, two of the company's senior directors and the secretary, Mr. Henry Davey, died.

Some time later, despite protests and appeals by the company and the Town Council, *the man with the knowledge*—namely the late Mr. Geoffrey Norman (brother of the writer)—was called up to join the Army as a private.

At that time the Allied Forces were advancing through Europe and there was an acute shortage of lorry drivers. *The man with the knowledge* was therefore given a two-week intensive course in lorry driving and then sent to France in convoy with a three-ton truck.

Meanwhile, back at Watchet, another plumber, who was above the age for call-up and the only one left in the town, did his very best to deal with all his own work plus emergency work for the company. The Town Council agreed to help by providing labourers when necessary.

A hot and very dry summer at that time caused a serious water shortage. Consequently town crier Albert Strong was sent around the town to announce that the company's water would be turned off each night to conserve supplies. Should there have been an outbreak of fire during the night, Mr. Billy Hunt, the captain of Watchet's Fire Brigade, had permission to turn the supply on again (up at the reservoir!). When water was seen oozing from the ground in Govier's Lane the Council sent two elderly labourers to dig out and locate the leaking water main.

The compacted metal in the lane was terribly hard and although the two old chaps dug and dug with their picks and shovels for a week, no main was located. A lot more water was then noticed oozing up in another part of the lane so another deep trench was dug. So it went on for over three weeks. The lane was in a shocking state. People were complaining and still no main was found.

During darkness red oil lamps were placed in position to warn pedestrians of the open trenches. These lights were soon spotted and extinguished by an over-zealous air-raid warden. He insisted that no lights whatever could be allowed during the blackout. "If they were," he said, "Watchet would be bombed to smithereens by the Luftwaffe."

After some poor old soul had stumbled after dark into one of the water-filled trenches, the water company, the Council and the police became quite concerned. It was agreed that an urgent message be sent to the commanding officer of Pte. Norman's unit to acquaint him of the problem and requesting him to contact Pte. Norman to telegraph back the whereabouts of the water main and, if possible, to allow him to return on leave. A prompt reply was received from the C.O. It read as follows:

"REGRET NO LEAVE POSSIBLE—STOP—HAVE CONTACTED NORMAN—STOP—HE STATES—SILLY FOOLS DIGGING IN WRONG PLACE—STOP—NO MAIN IN GOVIER'S LANE—STOP—MAIN RUNS THROUGH TEDDY DUDDRIDGE'S GARDEN ALONGSIDE LANE."

On receiving this vital information from *the man with the knowledge* Mr. Teddy Duddridge was quickly found and informed there was a water main in his garden which was believed to be leaking. "I could 'ave told 'ee that meself," he said. "Thic pipe 'ave been leaking for months—look at me gurt cabbages an' me prize kidney beans—they be the best in town!"

THE RIVALS

Those graceful schooners and ketches which in bygone days traded from Somerset ports live now only in the memory of the elderly.

Of these, the only one still sailing is the lovely ketch "IRENE"—the last ship to be built (1907) at Bridgwater. The "IRENE" is no longer in the cargo-carrying trade. Now, carefully restored to her original rig and with her cargo hold converted to living accommodation, she is available on charter to sailing enthusiasts.

Owned and under the command of Capt. Leslie Morrish, she visits many ports around Britain and the Continent, and returned recently from a spell in the Mediterranean. Wherever she sails she is admired for her graceful lines and ship-shape appearance. Long may she continue sailing.

In the early 1900s shipowners and sailors in all small ports took a great pride in their own particular ship. At that time, steamships being less dependent on weather conditions were gradually capturing more and more of the trade which traditionally had belonged to the sailing ships. There was, therefore, fierce competition and rivalry among sailing-ship men to obtain a share of the dwindling trade. Some masters would point out and perhaps exaggerate to shipping agents the fast sailing capabilities of their own vessel. Understandably they might belittle the competing ships from nearby ports.

At the port of Watchet the "KINGS OAK"—a fore and aft schooner owned by Capt. Richard Harris—was known to be a very fast sailing vessel. It was generally considered that she could outstrip any ship on the Somerset coast. Originally built as a Yarmouth sailing trawler in 1884, the "KINGS OAK" was very sharp in her hull form and was known to have sailed from Waterford in Ireland for Bridgwater in record-breaking time.

The newly-built "IRENE" also had very fine lines and was much admired by many mariners who saw her being built. "She'll have a tidy turn of speed," they said, "and she'll beat any Watchet vessel hands down." Sure enough, these rash words came to the ear of Capt. Harris at Watchet. A man of few words, Capt. Harris just smiled and said quietly, "We'll see about that". His few simple words, however, were rushed to Bridgwater where they were presented as a challenge to the captain of the "IRENE"—the race of the rivals was now unavoidable.

Whether by design or perhaps coincidence, it came about that the newly-built "IRENE" and the "KINGS OAK" (both loaded with bricks) were to sail from Bridgwater to Waterford on the same tide. There was great excitement among sailors in each port and bets were laid on the result of the race. By arrangement a telegram was sent on the day of the race to let Watchet sailors know when the ships were to set sail.

It all happened over eighty years ago. Ernest Binding—a young boy at the time and the son of a Watchet sailor—died only recently. He told the writer that he with his father and most of Watchet's seafaring men turned out to see the two ships racing down the Bristol Channel. Both ships could clearly be seen from Watchet's pier with all sails set in a very strong westerly breeze working their way to windward, each tacking to and fro. "It was a wonderful sight," said Ernest, "and one I have never forgotten."

As the ships disappeared from sight, Watchet sailors were chuckling happily. The "KINGS OAK" was well in the lead and still forging ahead. According to Ernest and several others with long memories, the race was won fairly and squarely by "KINGS OAK". Money changed hands, they said, and pints of beer were consumed in celebration. But Ernest's tale was disputed later by seafaring men of Bridgwater. Because the weather worsened, they told the writer, both ships had sought shelter in Milford Haven and the first ship to reach Waterford, they understood,

Kings Oak of Watchet painting by Reuban Chappel, owned by Mrs. N. Jilks.

was the "IRENE". "Well," said Ernest Binding with a shrug, "they would say that, wouldn't they?"

What is certain is that both these ships were well thought of by experienced mariners in each port—men who had the knowledge and ability to harness the power of the wind and tide. This was surely the time of 'wooden ships and iron men'.

There is rather a sad little sequel to this tale. In 1911 the "KINGS OAK" encountered heavy weather while on voyage from Liverpool for Bridgwater. On that fateful trip Capt. Harris had the harrowing experience of seeing one of his sons washed overboard and drowned. When the "KINGS OAK" returned to Watchet she had a blue band painted around her side—a sad custom at that time to indicate that their ship was in mourning.

In July 1923 when bound from Cardiff for New Ross in Ireland, the "KINGS OAK", due to stress of weather, attempted to put into Swansea for shelter. She stranded between the piers and was badly damaged. No lives were lost, but after being towed to Appledore, hopefully for repair, the "KINGS OAK" was condemned and broken up.

THE DEATH OF "NELSON"

One of the most hard-working and likeable men I ever knew was Arthur Rowe, of Watchet. He was a stalwart son of the soil who had spent his whole life with working horses. He loved and understood them. When I knew him in the 1930s Arthur owned two elderly Shire horses named "Captain" and "Nelson", and with their aid he earned a hard living as a haulage contractor. From the beach he hauled cartloads of shingle and sand, delivering them to building sites around the district. The laborious task of loading the cart with a shovel was done entirely by himself in all weathers.

Arthur also delivered loads of calcined limestones from kilns at Warren and Daws Castle. The stones, after slaking with water, were used by builders to make mortar and plaster. In season he ploughed or harrowed fields for smallholders, and also hauled loads of seaweed from the shore to spread on and fertilise the soil.

His happiest summertime task was taking wagon loads of children on Sunday School outings—often the only ones the kids ever had. On the return journey they and their teachers would lustily sing "God bless the horse and the driver for bringing us safely home". Arthur's rugged and weather-beaten face would break into a huge smile. It was all grist to the mill and he would cheerfully take on any work that came his way.

Arthur was blessed with a rich West Somerset dialect which he used generously and loudly to chide or encourage each horse in turn as it toiled. The variable tone of his gravelly voice was the bond of understanding between man and horse, and rarely did he strike either animal with a whip. Pulling in line, both horses would willingly haul the heavily-laden cart and work well together, but Nelson in particular did not take kindly to backing—often a difficult task, especially on building sites with mud nearly up to the axle. Sometimes the horse would become obstreperous, rear up and whinny in protest. Arthur had his own way in dealing with such tantrums—he would take hold of Nelson's bridle with both hands and push backwards. Man and horse, eyeball to eyeball, Arthur hollering "Git back! Git back! You silly gurt nughead!" Nelson always knew when he was beaten and hated being shouted at. With the cart correctly in position, Arthur would pat the horse affectionately and say, "Wull done, Nullson, wull done—thees can do it if thees try!"

Arthur had little faith in vets and possibly could not afford their fees. Should either horse require a drench, he would dispense his own medicine which he made by boiling certain wild herbs in water from St. Decuman's Holy Well. A vital ingredient was a spoonful or two of soot which had to come from the chimney of a woodburning fire. With the help of his friend, Ern Duddridge, and a device called a 'twitch' (necessary to keep the horse's mouth open), he would hoist the animal's

Mr. Arthur Rowe and his horse about to lead a Salvation Army Sunday School outing to Holford in 1908.

nose high in the air and, standing on a barrel, pour about a quart of the dark mixture down the invalid's throat. Meanwhile he would say soothingly, "Swaller it down, ther's a good 'orse. This'll put thee guts to rights an' make 'ee right as rain." If either horse was seriously ill, he had been known to stay with it in the stable at night to comfort it by his presence.

Arthur was also a Salvationist and a member of the Watchet Corps Band. Every Sunday he would don his uniform and march with the band to open-air street services proudly beating a large bass drum. Once he was asked to tell a Bible story at a service held on the Esplanade— how the boy David slew Goliath, the giant of the Philistines. "An' little David, he said loudly, "croupied down and picked up a stoan an'put'n in 'ees sling, an' then ee let fly . . .an' ee hat the ugly gurt twoad ass over 'ead an' killd'n stoan dead." Arthur's down to earth version was very much enjoyed and related around the town.

One day one of Arthur's horses died while grazing in a field and Arthur was told of this by a passer-by. At first he doubted if the horse was dead and said, "If'twas NulIson thees seed, 'ees likely as not asleep; 'ee do work 'ard like I, an' ee might wull 'av laid 'eeself down ver a nap." However, on going to the field Arthur found to his surprise and sorrow that Nelson had indeed passed away. "Wull I'll be jiggered, 'ee 'ave kicked the bucket" he said tearfully. "I never knowed the silly old nughead do that afore."

Next day he harnessed his surviving horse, "Captain," and on arrival at a building site was asked 'Where's Nelson?' "I doan rightly know," he replied sadly, "ee've left theas world an' I reckon 'ees now headin' up thic hill towards Zion."

After many years of hard work, Arthur retired. He and his horse could no longer compete with motor lorries, tractors and charabancs. All over the country the once familiar clip-clop of heavy working horses was fading away and, with them, the quaint wisdom and speech of their masters.

YANKEE JACK

When walking through Watchet's narrow Market Street, many visitors are intrigued by a name-plate on one of the neat little cottages. It reads 'Yankee Jack's Cottage'—and thereby hangs a tale, for in this charming cottage there once lived one of Watchet's most famous sailors, whose real name was John Short. Born in 1839, John grew up beside the harbour and,like many boys of that time, went to sea in one of the small coasting vessels trading to and from the port. He longed to travel and see

One of John Short's earliest ships was the last of the old East Indiamen, The Earl of Balcarres.

the world and while in his 'teens, shipped aboard the brig *Promise*, bound for the Spanish port of Cadiz. From there the brig sailed on to Quebec and John decided that this was the life for him.

Sailors knew that the arduous and often monotonous work aboard ship could be helped along by singing rhythmic choruses known as sea shanties. John, having a good strong voice, readily joined in the singing which he greatly enjoyed. He travelled all over the world in a variety of sailing ships and learned the words and tunes of dozens of shanties, often taking the 'lead' part for himself. This required a fair measure of musical skill to ensure that the timing of the music and the words fitted the particular work in hand.

In the early 1860s John served aboard ships running the blockade in the American Civil War and it was because of his service in these ships that he was given the nickname of 'Yankee Jack' by Watchet sailors. John did not resent this nickname which he knew to be complimentary and given with affection. In the 1880s John's wife was taken ill and he came back to Watchet to be at her side. Just occasionally he sailed again on short coastal voyages. He never owned or took command of any ship. He was an 'Able Seaman' and in that capacity was highly skilled and second to none.

In 1914, Cecil Sharp, a well-known collector of English folk-songs and shanties, realised that 'lead' shantymen were very few and far between. He had searched all over Britain in order to collect the words and music of traditional British sea shanties, in order to record them for posterity. His search for shantymen in the docklands of many large ports proved disappointing, producing only the odd shanty here and there. Continuing his search in the smaller ports, he made his greatest discovery at Watchet, where John Short was willing to sing to him a great variety of British and American shanties, most of which Sharp had never heard of before. He was immensely impressed with John's voice which he declared to be, 'Rich, resonant and powerful, yet so flexible that he can execute trills, turns and graces with a delicacy and finish that would excite the envy of many a professional vocalist'. A few years later Sir Richard Terry, another collector, also recorded John's authentic songs of the sea which were willingly sung again and again.

At all times a straight-forward and God-fearing man, John was quite unaffected by the many visits of these two eminent gentlemen and the fame they brought him. He continued to live without fuss in his little cottage near the harbour and was often called on by neighbours and friends to sing at local concerts.

John Short lived until he was 94 and was active and still singing until a few weeks before his death in 1933. A brief and simple obituary notice in *The Times* said of Watchet's grand old sailor, 'He thought little of his reputation as a singer, but much more of homely things'.

John Short, of Watchet (Yankee Jack).

53

THE GHOSTS OF WATCHET TOWN
(A Song)

Words and Music by Derek Quint

1. Listen very carefully
    When walking through the narrow street
    The narrow street called Market Street in Watchet Town;
    There's cobble stones beneath your feet,
    There's cottages small, trim and neat
    A history that is bitter sweet in Watchet Town;
    And you may just hear the singing
    Of Yankee Jack ringing in your ears,
    Yes you may just hear him singing
    Though Yankee Jack's been dead for many years.

2. Listen very carefully
When walking past the London Inn
Towards the lighthouse on the pier in Watchet Town;
Picture times of long ago
When sailing ships would come and go
And sailors told of joy and woe in Watchet Town;
And you may just hear reciting
The voice of Coleridge gentle in your ears
His "Rime of The Ancient Mariner",
A tale of superstition and of fear.

3. Listen very carefully
When walking through the narrow street
The narrow street called Market Street in Watchet Town;
There's a little café there
It's said it has a tunnel where
The smugglers used to hide their wares in Watchet Town;
And you may just hear the whispering
From the passages below
Yes you may just hear them whispering
Though it's said that smuggling ended years ago.

4. Listen very carefully
When visiting the local inns,
The "Anchor", "London", "Star" and "Bell" in Watchet Town;
You'll hear tales of olden times
You'll hear about the mineral line
And men who came down from the mines to Watchet Town;
And you may just hear them shouting
Or laughing as they spend their pay
It's said that there was fighting
But the mines all lie in ruins there today.

5. Wander now and look around
For you will see a busy town,
A harbour and a little train in Watchet Town;
Life goes on and so it will
A busy port and paper mill,
But history will linger still in Watchet Town;
And you may just hear the singing
Or the whispering or the rhyme
Of the sailors, the smugglers or the miners,
The ghosts of Watchet from a bygone time.

By the same author:

'TALES OF WATCHET HARBOUR'

ISBN 0 95108 42 0 8